Welcome To Wall Street 101

A Beginner's Manual to Stocks, Trading, & Investing

Ramon Singleton

Welcome to Wall Street 101: A Beginner's Manual to Stocks, Trading, & Investing

Printed in the United States of America

ISBN: 978-0-578-33666-4

DEDICATION

This book is dedicated to my mentor Mr. Tony A. Walker for being such a great teacher, leader and role model to so many young brothers that's incarcerated behind the walls and searching for a way to turn their lives around in such a positive way! You are truly a blessing to me and many others. I want to thank Natelisha Jackson for all your help, support and love for backing me in all of my endeavors. Ron and Doretha G. Baldwin for helping me with this project. Thanks a bunch! Lastly, Ms. Arnesjah Miller, you've been such a blessing to me throughout this process and I greatly appreciate your patience and time you've dedicated to making my dreams into reality with this project. Thanks so much and I look forward to working with you on many more projects in the future. God bless all and I hope y'all enjoy the read and learn something that'll help you along the way with your trading journey.

TABLE OF CONTENTS

INTRODUCTION

Hi, and Welcome to this Wonderful World of Trading and Investing in the Stock Market. In this book we will cover all of the basic things you will need to know about the Stock Market. We will also dig into some of the more advanced factors involved in some of the more advanced factors when it comes to trading and investing into the Stock Market. So, Relax, Unwind and Let's Drop Some New Knowledge into Your Mind.

CHAPTER 1

Let's Talk Market

Stock is equity position in a company's ownership. In other words, you own a piece of that company when you buy shares/stocks in that particular company. Plain and simple.

When someone hears the words "Stock Market" or "Wall Street", these are two words that almost all investors and the average "Joe Blow" think of. They are also somewhat familiar with the term "The Dow Jones".

From top professionals down to the guys and girls that have not traded a single penny, will have their opinion on our stock market. So, best believe The Dow Jones will most likely be mentioned in their conversation.

So, in this chapter, I will introduce to you The Dow Jones, S&P 500, NASDAQ, and NYSE. This will give you some insight and basic understanding, but powerful knowledge about these indexes.

The DOW Jones

What is the Market doing? Where is the Market at? Where did the Market close? Are we in a Bull or Bear Market?

There are only a few questions you will hear talked about and discussed daily when dealing with not only the financial markets but our overall economy as well. That one thing people will turn to for those answers listed above – is the Dow Jones. How is the Dow performing? Great question, and it is one you should know the answer to if you plan on trading or investing in The Markets.

Let's break the Dow Jones down for better understanding; the Dow is the oldest index and has been around since 1882. The Dow Jones holds 30 Blue Chip stocks and gives us a gauge of our overall market and economy as well. These 30 Blue Chips stocks are household names used that you may have heard of before such as American Express, Apple, CAT, Home Depot, Johnson & Johnson, Coca-Cola, JP Morgan Chase, McDonald's, Microsoft, Nike, Visa, Wal-Mart, and Walt Disney just to name a few.

NOTE: You cannot buy stock from the Dow Jones, you will purchase these stocks through other indexes; however, you can follow and trade the DOW (DJIA) and purchase it through an exchange-traded fund (ETF). An EFT is a basket security (stocks and/or other financial instruments) that is traded on an exchange. EFT's are a safer investment than investing in a single stock. They are not usually as volatile as individual stocks which makes them a safer investment and a great long-term investment.

The S&P 500

(Standard and Poor's 500)

The S&P 500 is a publicly-traded index that tracks 500 of the U.S. largest companies.

The 500 companies traded on the SnP 500 give us a healthy gauge of the overall health of these 500 large companies, which in return gauges the strength of America's top 500 companies. The S&P 500 is probably the most popular index in the world and is used as a performance benchmark for a variety of mutual funds, ETF's and other assets and securities. In short, The S&P 500 acts as a barometer of the entire US stock market, and many firms, funds, and analysts compare their performance against the S&P 500 over a certain period of time (weekly, monthly, quarterly, bi-annual, annually).

NASDAQ

National Association of Securities Dealers
Automated Quotations
Nickname: Tech Heavy

The NASDAQ is the second-largest stock exchange globally based on the market capitalization of listed companies (exceeded only by the NYSE).

Most stocks are technology or internet related and that's how it received the nickname "Tech Heavy". However, there are also financial, industrial, biotech, and consumer companies listed on the NASDAQ as well.

The NASDAQ tracks more than 3,300 companies and has a market cap of 19.5 trillion dollars.

Most of the stocks you purchase will come either from the NASDAQ or the NYSE.

NOTE: The NASDAQ market began in 1971 and was the first electronic stock market. While the NYSE still trades on the floor/pits.

NYSE

New York Stock Exchange

On May 17, 1792, is when Twenty-Four stockbrokers signed the Buttonwood Agreement on Wall Street; and that is when the NYSE was founded. However, it wasn't until 25 years later that the organization officially became the New York Stock Exchange Board.

The NYSE is the largest equities-based exchange in the world, based on the total Market Capitalization of its listed stocks and other securities. There are over 2,800 companies that are listed on the NYSE that are trading 1.6 billion shares each day.

CHAPTER 2

Fundamentals

Here I will explain to you the Fundamental Principles of investing and trading. I will also give you a broad view of how to read all of those crazy numbers that you've seen crammed in various sections of the Newspapers. Some of you may have thought, at some point in life they were difficult to read or understand.
By the time you are done with this chapter, I am quite sure you will feel as though you have learned a lot and you're almost ready to begin investing. So, Sit Back and Enjoy!
There are two ways an investor may choose to invest: Fundamental Investing and Technical Analysis

- Fundamental Investing focuses on the economic forces of supply and demand that cause prices to move higher, stay the same, or drop lower.
- Technical Analysis studies and concentrates on the study of Market action. I will explain more of the technical analysis in the next chapter.

When someone studies the fundamentals of a company, they are usually concerned with what is going on inside the company such as:

- New Products being Released
- New CEO or key Player or Investor(s) that is joining the Company
- Is the Company Expanding or Growing?
- Are there any lawsuits against the company?
- What are the Company's expectations for the future?
- Most importantly what does the Company's Books or Records Reveal

These are all great things that investors and potential investors should take into consideration when investing and using the fundamental principles. Lucky, these things can be easily found with just a click of a button or two. Or, simply turning the pages in your choice of newspaper you invest from. Let's Read the Newspaper.

This Photo by Unknown Author is licensed under CC BY-NC-ND

SYM/TICK

This is an Abbreviation of the "Company's Name", sort of like a nickname.

Example	**Symbol**
Montel Mobile Laundry Service	MMLS
Get Fyne Fitness	GFF
Dog Tooth Dentist	DTD
Orange Florida T	OFLT

Usually, NASDAQ has 4 letters and NYSE usually has 3 letters for their ticker symbol.

52 WEEK HIGH

This is the Highest Price that stock has reached within the past 52 weeks (1 Year)

52 WEEK LOW

This is the Lowest Price that stock has reached within the past 52 weeks (1 Year)

LAST/CLOSE

The Last/Close is the closing price in which that stock is traded at the end of that session. Simply Said – When the U.S. Stock Market Close @ 4:00 pm EST, whatever that Stock Closed for at the end of the day will be the Stock Last/Close.

CHG %

This will be how much either that stock has gained or lost % percentage-wise compared to its last trading period. Three examples on each:

3.8% 1.8% 14.27% -7.6% -.03% -17.92

Positive/Up Negative/Down

NOTE: This time frame is usually measured in days. However, it can be calculated on a weekly, monthly, and yearly basis. The time frame can go longer but is usually not needed unless you are planning on long-term investing.

VALUE CHANGE/CHG

This is the Dollar ($) or Change (cents) amount that has closed in since its last recorded trading period. This is the Dollar $ or Change (cents).

Example #1: Yesterday XYZ closed at 7.60
Today XYZ closed at 7.20

Example #2:
You have a change of .40 or -.40
Yesterday DTXX closed at 4.00

Example #3: Today DTXX closed at 5.15
You have a CHG of. 1.15

VOL (Volume)

Volume in broadly speaking about investing simply means the total amount of a Share exchanged (bought/sold) over a recorded period i.e., Daily, Weekly, Monthly, Yearly, etc.

Example: Company XYZ

Mutual Fund DTYZ	Bought	100,000 shares of XYZ today
Mutual Fund YT25	Sold	250,000 shares of XYZ today
Joe Blow	Bought	1,000
Total Shares Sold/Bought/Traded		351,000 shares of XYZ today
Daily Volume		351,000

RS (RELATIVE STRENGTH)

Relative Strength is a tool/indicator used to compare a benchmark or stock against another. Basically, you are comparing a stock against stocks in its sector or similar to it. A rising RS is good. NOTE: RS can also be compared against other broader factors; such as the DOW/NASDAQ/S&P/Mutual Funds/Hedge Funds, etc.

YTD (YEAR-TO-DATE)

Year to Date (YTD) shows the Performance of a stock over a One-Year Calendar Period up to the current date.

Example: Jan. 1, 2019 to Jan. 1, 2020: XYZ is up 8% YTD

Example of YTCX Stock		**Example Stock TXYA**	
Jan 1, 2019	2.00 Price	Jan 2, 2001	5.75 Price
Jan 1, 2020	2.20 Price	Jan 2, 2002	5.50 Price
YTD	up 20% or .20	YTD	down -.04% OR .25

SECTORS/INDUSTRIES

Each Group Stock falls into a Sector and then into an Industry. I will explain the difference and break down the two. A Sector is a Group of companies (stocks) that are similar and react similarly to one another in given economic conditions. After a stock falls into a sector group, it is then broken down into categories by the industrial group to narrow its category down to a micro-level. Examples:

Stock	**Sector**	**Industry**
Goldman Sachs	Financials	Banks
Walmart	Consumer Discretion	Retail
Pfizer	Health Care	Pharmaceutical
AAPL	Technology	Computers
Verizon	Telecom	Wireless Provider

There are 11 Sectors and 197 Industries. To list all sectors and industries would take an enormous amount of time, but here are a few:

Sectors	**Industries**
Technology	Media
Information	Agriculture
Health Care	Food
Utilities	Construction
Real Estate	Transport
Materials	Pharmaceuticals
Energy	Chemicals
	Infrastructure

MARKET-CAP

Here I will discuss the stocks and which Market Capitalization Range they fall under. Market Capitalization is a term that represents the total value that the market places on a company. You can find a company's market cap by multiplying the number of outstanding shares by the stock price. For the sale of this book, we will only cover the three (3) main Market Caps, but I will give you examples of others.

1	2	3
LARGE CAP	MID CAP	SMALL CAP

These are the main market caps you will be hearing and reading about constantly. So, let's get a little more familiar with each.

Large Cap Stocks are valued @ $10 billion and up
Mid Cap Stocks are valued @ $2 billion - $10 billion
Small Cap Stocks are valued @ $300 million - $2 billion

Others are Micro and Mega Caps

As previously mentioned at the beginning of this chapter these tools discussed in this chapter are more so for understanding the basic fundamental principles of investing and understanding how to read the newspapers and giving you a broad view of what that company has done or projected to do over a certain period of time.

CHAPTER 3

Technical Analysis

Technical Analysis concentrates on the study of the markets and technicians use chart patterns and other indicators they have set to help them buy, sell and trade stocks and other securities. These individuals are called technicians and usually have some form of knowledge of fundamental investing. Although, the fundamentalist doesn't always have the knowledge or skills of technical investing/ trading.

Most technicians usually trade and invest in stocks in a shorter timeframe than those who use fundamentals do. Their goal is to get in and out of a stock before it hits the news, newspaper, or media and exit with a profit.

Technical investing/trading can be much more fun, exciting and profitable if you become good at this skill and take it seriously. These individuals catch the market moves a lot earlier than the fundamentalist and the masses and by the time everyone else hears about the great news or movement of a stock the technician is usually already in and out of that particular security.

Technical investing is definitely where the money is at!!! And now I'll show you a few charts and tools that technicians keep at their disposal to help them enter and exit trades.

$INDU Dow Jones Industrial Average INDX (DAILY)

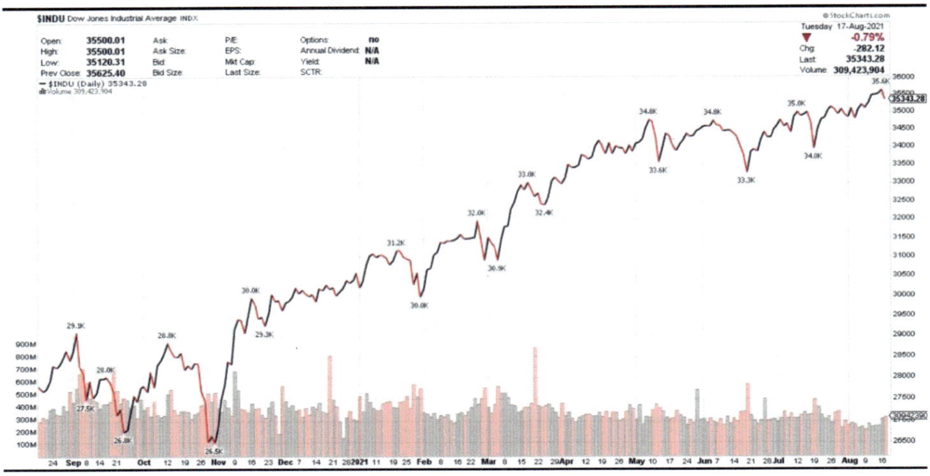

Here is a line chart of the Dow Jones Industrial Average (INDU). These line charts are very simple to read on a basic level. The black lines are price movements in the upward/bullish direction, and the red lines are prices moving in the downward direction.

Over to the very right side of the chart is the price increments. The numbers to the very left side of the chart are the volume increments. The Red/Black bars at the bottom of the chart are the volume.

NOTE: All charts can be read in many different time frames such as minutes, hours, days, weekly, etc. Above is a daily chart of the Dow Jones Industrial Average and below is a monthly chart of the Dow Jones Industrial Average. The two charts look different because they are shown in two different time frames.

$INDU Dow Jones Industrial Average Index

Here is that same daily chart of the Dow Jones Industrial Average only now in a candlestick form, rather than a line chart. These candlestick charts are a little more difficult to read because they produce multiple patterns that predict the future price movement of these stocks/securities. However, for the purpose of this book, I'll keep the reading of these charts simple, but on the next page and later in this chapter I will explain candlestick reading a little more in-depth.

The price and volume increments are read the same as the bar chart. The white days on the chart are bullish days, meaning the stock/security closed higher than it opened.

The red/black days are the opposite. The stock opened and at the end of the day, it closed lower than it opened, meaning it was a Bearish day. The tails/shadows at the bottom of each candlestick are the low for that day. The tails/shadows at the top of the candlestick are the highest for that day.

NOTE: These candlestick charts can also be traded and read in many different time frames such as minutes, hours, daily, weekly, etc.

CANDLESTICK charting offers you a more clear and vivid picture of what happened (price-wise) on a chart than on a Line Chart. Line charts are usually tracked by a closing price for whatever particular time period. However, Candle Sticks show the Open, High, Low, and Close for that recorded time period.

A candle has two parts: The Body and The Shadow

1. The Body of the candle is the Open and Close (See example below).
2. The Shadow is the High and Low of the candle (See example below).

If the Candle is white the stock closes higher than it opened. It was a Bullish Day. If the Candle is black then the stock closes lower than it opened. It was a Bearish Day. Candles throw off many different patterns and these patterns must be learned. Examples 1 and 2 are considered long days due to the length of the candle body. Example 3 is a short doji day because of the short body.

Example #1 **Example #2**

Bullish Candle **Bearish Candle**

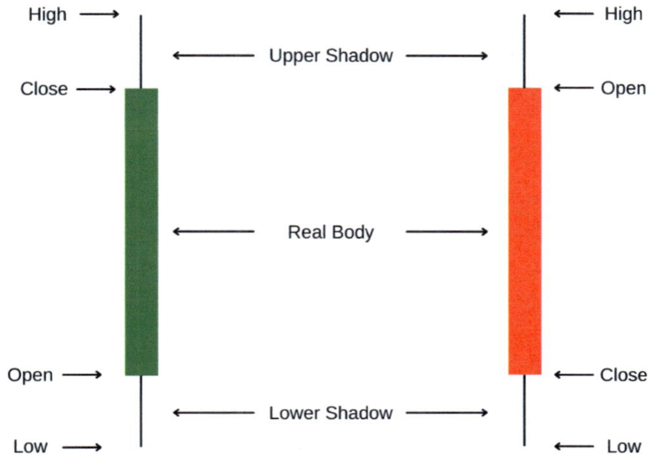

Example #3

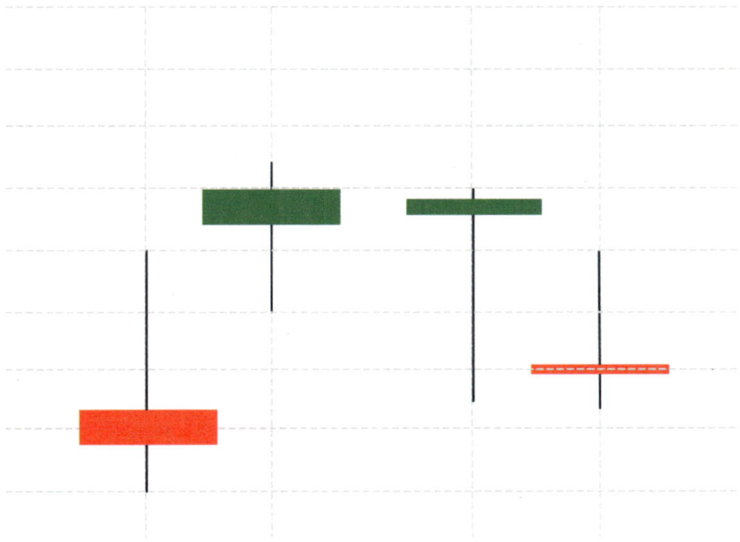

These are smaller days or “doji” days.

$INDU Dow Jones Industrial Average Index —

This is a bar chart of the same stock The Dow Jones Industrial Average.

Price and volume increments are read the same as the previous charts.

The red days are bearish/down days.

The black days are bullish/up days.

The bar to the left side is open.

The bar to the right side is the close.

The low is the bottom of the bar.

The high is the top of the bar.

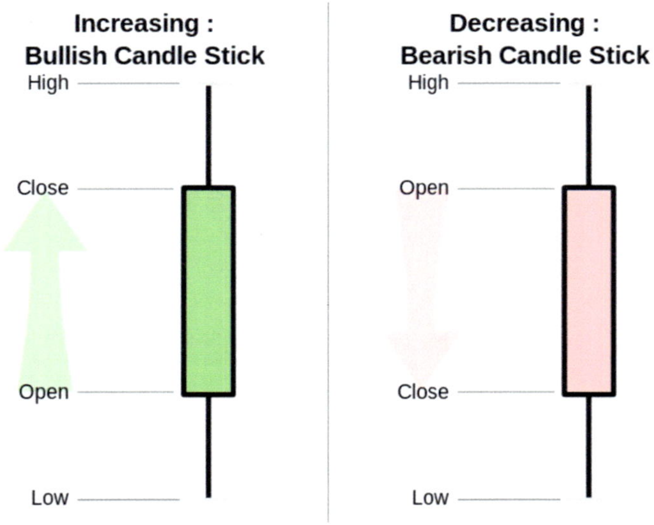

Now that you have some basic knowledge of chart reading, I will explain two very important key components that you will need to know: Support and Resistance. I will also show you how to identify those important areas online, candlestick, and bar charts.

<u>**Support**</u> - A bottom or a price area that a bottom or a price area that a stock has fallen to in the past. This does not necessarily have to be a stock's bottom

<u>**Resistance**</u> - A top or previous high area that a stock has risen to before turning down. This does not necessarily have to be stocks top or all-time high.

*See charts on the next few pages to get a clearer visual of Support and Resistance.

FCEL Fuel Cell Energy Chart

Support and Resistance on a Line Chart Support and Resistance on a Candlestick Chart NOTE: Support and Resistance can also be read by using the Highs and Lows on a Candlestick Chart or Bar Chart

FCEL Fuel Cell Energy Chart

Support and Resistance on a Bar Chart NOTE: Support and Resistance get a lot deeper than I have discussed here in the book. These two factors play a very important role in a stock Reversal and I suggest you read more on the two every chance you get!

Stock Chart Candlestick Patterns

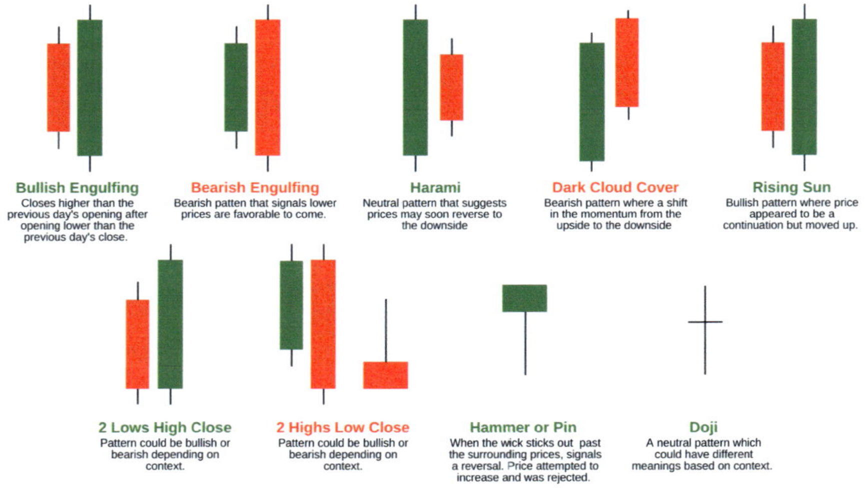

Here's how to read a candlestick and also a few candlestick patterns you will see quite often on charts.

NOTE: There are dozens of other candlestick patterns that you need to learn to be proficient at recognizing and trading while using these candlestick charts.

Believe it or not, we've covered a lot in this third (3rd) chapter dealing with technical analysis, but there are a few more key jewels I must add to complete this chapter.

We know what a stock is: equity position in a company. Now you need to know that stocks move in three trends.

1) Uptrend
2) Downtrend
3) Sideways trend or Consolidation

An Uptrend is a series of successive higher highs and higher lows. (See FCEL CHART)

A Downtrend is a series of successive lower lows and lower highs. (See FCEL CHART)

A Sideways Trend or Consolidation period is when a stock moves sideways without forming an up or downtrend.

FCEL CHART

FCEL CHART

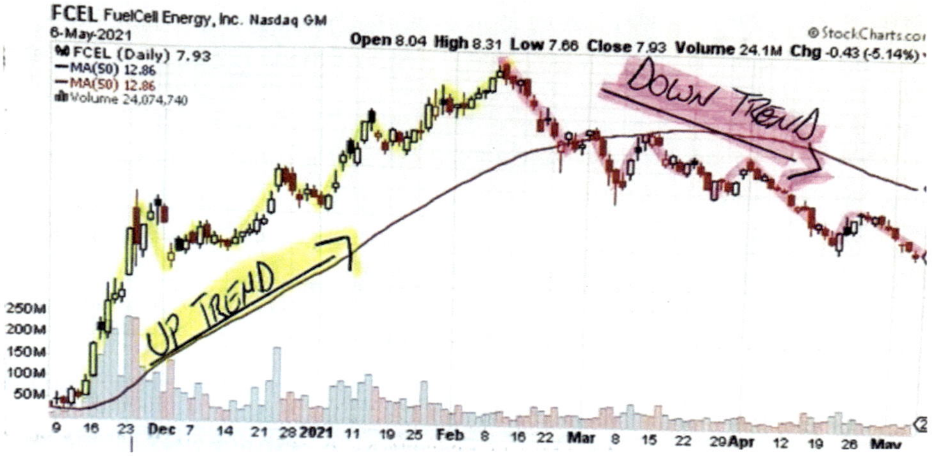

Now that you understand the three trends and support and support and resistance I'll explain the three premises that most if not all technicians approach the market with before executing their trades whether it be buying or selling. These three premises are often referred to as Dow Theory.

1. Price action discounts everything. Meaning technicians believe that everything they need to know about that stock is factored into the price (usually the closing price of that stock). They believe that price action will be the first indication of that stock's future movement. All they need to know will be factored into that price action and they'll get an early signal before the masses.
2. Prices move in three trends (up, down, or sideways). These are the only three ways a stock can move.
3. History repeats itself. Meaning if a stock has been at that price range before, then it's a great chance it'll return to that price level and visit it once again.

CHAPTER 4

How to Open a Trading Account

Now that you've taken the time out to read this entire book, it's only right that I explain to you step by step how to open up a trading account so you can get the dough rolling in. Choosing a broker can be tricky and quite complex but here in this example, we'll use **Etrade** because their website is easy to navigate and their customer service is always excellent! Plus, they're great with entering and exiting your trades!!! So, let's jump right to it!

1. The very first thing you will need to do is set your account up as an INDIVIDUAL ACCOUNT. This is self-explanatory and is simply an account that one person (you) will be listed on and controlling.
2. Next, you'll need to enter your contact information: name, phone number, and email address.
3. Your personal information will need to be provided: Country, address, zip code, city, and state.
4. Identity Verification is next: DOB and SSI #.
5. Employment details: In this section, you'll choose your employment/employer. Note: If you are employed, choose your occupation and list all of their information in the boxes.
6. Investment Profile: The first box I usually fill in with GROWTH as my investment objective although it doesn't matter which answer you choose to fill in the box. The other boxes will be filled in with annual income, liquid net worth, total net worth, investment experience, marital status, and number of dependents. (For this section I just filled in the blanks to give you examples but each person's income, net worth, etc. will be different).
7. Regulatory Questions: Are all usually answered NO because these are questions basically asking if you or a family member is a member of the board of directors of a publicly-traded

company, own 10% or more of a publicly-traded company, or work for a broker/dealer.

8. Brokerage Account Basics: These two questions are basically how will you fund this account? And the purpose and expected use of this account. For this example, I choose savings and active/day trading.
9. Brokerage Account Setup: Simply choose the first ones as I have in this example.
10. Agreements and Disclosures: Review this information carefully and just agree to these terms (plain and simple).
11. And just like that SUBMIT the application and your account is ready to go!!!!

With your account now open it's 3 questions you need to ask yourself.

Question #1: "Do I have a plan?"
A plan and discipline are the keys to successful trading over a long period of time. Create a plan, stick to it and be sure to cut losses quickly. Not all trades will go in your favor and you MUST understand that. The key is to take your losses and move on to the next trade. Dwelling on your losses will not get your money back, in fact, it will only have your head and your judgment will not be clear for future trades. So, have a plan, stick to it and remember even the greatest traders take losses.

Question #2: "How much money do I need to start with to fund my account?"
This is a question I can't answer for you. Only you know what you can stand to invest or lose. Everyone's starting point will be different but I advise anyone who's an intermediate to begin small ($25.00-$100.00). The reason being is because this trading thing is an emotional game! People love to win but hate to lose money and as I stated earlier, you will definitely take some losses. Starting small will allow you to get the feel of the market without taking too much risk. Sure, your wins won't be as large but your losses won't be as great either. Remember, you're in this for the long haul. Wallstreet is not a

get-rich-quick scheme. Just like with success in everything else you do in life this too will take time and patience. So, I advise you to start small, practice daily, and be patient. Consistency is key!!!

Question #3: "How long should I invest in the market?"
The last thing I'd advise a beginner to do is to invest for the long term (1 month or greater). However, if your stock reaches your specific selling point sooner than expected, then go ahead and exit that trade. But if not, stick to the plan and see if your analysis turns out to be correct. Give yourself some time in the stock. Study the stock and see how it acts to market news. What you want to consider is how it trades on a daily basis. Does it produce a lot of long candle patterns or short candle patterns? Does it move with the Dow, Nasdaq, or SNP? What is the volume doing? STUDY, STUDY, STUDY that's the key.

Good luck on your trading journey. I hope that this book helps you along the way and I wish you great success! If you would like to learn more techniques to win in the stock market, visit momentummonsters.com.

CHAPTER 5

Acronyms, Abbreviations, Definitions

Here are a few acronyms, abbreviations, and definitions you need to know. So, when you see them you will understand exactly what they mean.

Banking, Investing, Insurance, Role as a Citizen

Acronyms, Abbreviations

ATM	Automatic Teller Machine
CD	Certification of Deposit
CFP	Certified Financial Planner
CPI	Consumer Price Index
DJIA	Dow Jones Industrial Average
EPS	Earnings Per Share
FDIC	Federal Deposit Insurance Corporation
GDP	Gross Domestic Product
HMP	Health Maintenance Organization
IBD	Investor's Business Daily
IPO	Initial Public Offering
IRA	Individual Retirement Account
NASDAQ	National Association of Securities Dealers Quotation
NAV	Net Asset Value
OTC	Over The Counter
P&L	Profit and Loss (statement)
REIT	Real Estate Investment Trust
ROI	Return on Investment
S&P	Standard & Poor's
SEC	Securities Exchange Commission

Economics

Business Economic Cycle - Recurring periods of expansion (recovery) and contraction (recession) in economic activity with effects on inflation, growth, and employment.

CPI - A market basket of goods and services compiled monthly by the Bureau of Labor Statistics which reflects current economic trends and is widely used as a measure of inflation.
Depression - Economic conditions where money is extremely tight causing the economy to virtually stop – unemployment escalates, business collapses and the general mood is grim. A downturn in economic activity, defined as at least consecutive quarters of decline in a country's Gross Domestic Product.
Recovery - Period in the economic cycle when economic activity picks up and the Gross Domestic Product grows, leading into the expansion phase of the cycle.

Capitalization

Small-Caps	Companies with capitalization of less than $2 billion
Mid-Caps	Companies with capitalization between $2 billion and $10 billion
Large-Caps	Companies with capitalization of more than $10 billion

Categories of Investment*

a. Securities
b. Retirement Plans
c. Real Estate
d. Tangible Assets
e. Business Ventures

Investing

Amex	American Stock Exchange.
Annual Report	Yearly record of a corporation's financial condition that must be distributed to shareholders under SEC regulations.

Arbitrage	Making a profit by trading the same security, currency, or commodity in two or more markets simultaneously taking advantage of their prices and market timing.
Bear Market	A declining market, when stock prices drop rather sharply; pessimism, growing unemployment and sometimes a recession are common.
Bond	An IOU that a corporation or government agency issues when it wants to borrow money. The issuer agrees to pay back the lender at a specified maturity date, with interest.
Bull Market	An advancing market, where stock prices and everything else is on the upswing .
Bullion	Gold or silver in the form of bars or ingots.
Capital	Money used for business purposes; the reason corporations issue stock
Capital Gains	Any money you make from an investment, such as from selling stock for a profit. If you hold the investment longer than one year, any profit would be taxed at a rate lower than the regular income tax rate.
Commodities	Any products sold in the financial markets that can actually be weighed, such as gold, silver, pork bellies, sugar, or gain.
Contrarian	An investor who does the opposite of what most investors are doing at any particular time.
Discount Broker	Broker who simply executes trades, for a lower commission and without the additional services provided by a full-service broker.
Diversification	A Method of decreasing risk by increasing the variety of assets in a portfolio, such as owning many different stocks and funds. Do not put all your eggs in one basket.

Due Diligence	Professional responsibility that attention has been made to the business matters at hand to prevent mishandling or negligence.
Equity	Ownership of property, such as stock or a house.
Euro Dollars	Deposits of U.S. dollars at banks and other financial institutions outside the United States, especially in Europe.
Fortune 500	Annual listing by Fortune magazine of the 500 largest U.S. industrial corporations, ranked by sales.
Future	Contract to make a specific trade at a specified future date and future price (highly speculative).
Inflation	The gradual increases in the cost of living.
Institutional Investor	A large entity, such as a corporation, hospital, city government, insurance company, or pension fund, which has a portfolio.
Liquidity	The presence of buyers and sellers for a security, thus the ability to get money for the security quickly.
Market Maven	An expert on the workings of markets and investments.
Money Market	Market for short-term debt instruments which possess safety and liquidity.
Mutual Fund	Investing company whose business is to invest pools or investors' money gathered by the selling of its shares.
NASDAQ	An automated information network and exchange that provides quotes (prices) on stocks for brokers registered with NASD.
NYSE	The Big Board, largest stock exchange by capitalization in the world.
Option	Contract that gives the right – but not the obligation – to buy or sell a certain quantity of stocks or bonds, indexes, or future contracts.
OTC	Any trade not done on an exchange.

Portfolio	The mix of assets in which one has invested. It contains investment instruments that have been selected to achieve one's financial goals.
Risk	Any chance of loss.
S&P 500	Market index incorporates a broad base of 500 stocks (capitalization comprising approx. 87% of the corporate stock markets in the U.S. and is widely considered the benchmark for large-stock investments.
SEC	Government agency charged with regulating the securities industry.
Securities	Rightful claims to assets represented in a verifiable way, as on paper or computer records.
Speculation	A risk taken in order to achieve a greater return.
Stocks	Securities representing an ownership in a corporations' undivided assets.
The Fed	The Federal Reserve Board, the governing board of the Federal Reserve System.
The Street	The opinions and predictions of the investment community in general, but specifically, major brokerage houses and media investment gurus.
Wall Street	The investment community in general; common name for the financial district at the lower end of Manhattan in New York City.
Yield	The return of an investment expressed as a percentage.
Stocks	
Blue Chips	Stocks of the largest, long-established companies that are known for superior management and are consistently profitable offering investors stable and predictable income with steady if slow growth in value.
Common Stock	Stocks that share directly in the success or failure of a business.

Cyclical Stocks	Stocks that move in the same direction as the business cycle; stocks heavily influenced by the economy.
Day Trader	An investor that buys and sells the same security, (usually stock) closing out his position in one trading day.
Dividends	Portion of corporate earnings distributed to shareholders.
Dow Jones Industrial Average	Priced-weighted average of 30 activity traded blue chip stocks, primarily industrials but including service industries.
Fundamental Analysis	Analysis based on studying balance sheets, P&L statements and annual reports of a company thus determining the real value of a company's stock.
Going Public	The first time a company officially issues stock on the open market.
Insider Trading	Stock trades made by key employees such as directors, and corporate officers, who have access to information not made public yet.
Investment Bankers	Professionals who agree to underwrite an IPO.
IPO	The first sale offering of a stock.
Limit Order	Order to buy or sell stock at a pre-set limit price or better.
Losers	Stocks that posted losses for the day.
Margin	Cash used to purchase securities supplied with credit given by the broker.
Market Order	Order to buy or sell stock at the best possible price on the market.
Nikkei	Stock index that tracks the Tokyo stock exchange.
Odd Lot	Less than 100 shares of stock.
P\E Ratio	Price earnings ratio, measure whether a stock is overvalued or undervalued.
Penny Stocks	Stocks generally sold for $5 or less (historically, 80% fail to zero within 5 years).

Preferred Stock	Stocks where dividends are fixed and are paid before common stock with the added rights to assets during bankruptcy before common stock.
Rally	A quick rise in the market following a decline in the general price level.
Resistance	Technical indicator by which a stock's price historically tends to peak.
Round Lot	100 shares of stock.
Selling Short	Selling borrowed stocks at current prices and pocketing the money, then waiting for the price to fall, buying the shares and returning the stocks to the broker. The investor keeps the difference as profit.
Stock Split	Stock division that increases the number or shares outstanding and decreases share price (used to attract buyers).
Story Stock	Stock of a new company without real earnings, but with an exciting idea, opportunity, or technology.
Support	Technical indicator showing where a stock's price historically bottoms out.
Technical Analysis	Analysis based on charts that show price movements and volatility to determine the best time to buy and/or sell a security.
Trend	General direction of stock price (as plotted on a chart).
Value Line Investment Survey	Report of a company's business background, current happenings, information from financial statements, and stock performance provided by research company Value Line.
Volatility	The tendency of security prices to fluctuate.
Volume	Total number of shares traded during a given period.
Winners	Stocks that posted gains for the day.

Bonds

Agency Bonds	Bonds issued by mortgage associations nicknamed Ginnie Mae, Fannie Mae, and Freddie Mac, as well as federal and state agencies.
Corporate Bonds	Bonds issued by for-profit corporations.
Junk Bonds	Bonds of extremely low or no credit quality (high risk)
Municipal Bonds	Bonds issued by state and local governments.
Treasury Bills	Federal government debt securities with terms of 13 to 52 weeks; major component in the money market.
Treasury Bonds	Federal government debt securities with terms of 10 to 30 years.
Treasure Notes	Federal government debt securities with terms of 2 to 10 years.
U.S. Saving Bonds	Federal government bearer bonds which are issued in denominations, sold at a discount, and are not marketable.

Mutual Funds

Balanced Fund	Mutual fund that buys a mixture of stocks and bonds with the investment objective of providing a balance of growth and income.
Closed-end Fund	Mutual fund that issues a limited number of shares.
Dollar Cost Averaging	Investing a fixed dollar amount on a periodic schedule (usually each month), thereby averaging the purchases of shares over the long haul.
Global Fund	Mutual Fund which invests in markets located in other countries as well as in the U.S.
Green Fund	Mutual Fund that only buys shares of stock from environmentally conscious companies.
Growth Fund	Mutual fund that pursues speculative investments, such as stocks from small emerging companies,

	which present opportunities of aggressive financial growth.
Income Fund	Mutual Fund that invests in dividend-bearing stocks and short-term bonds to provide income to their shareholders.
Index Fund	Mutual Funds are designed to produce the same return that you would get if you owned all the stocks of a particular index, such as the S&P 500.
Load	Sales fees and commissions charged to investors in a mutual fund.
Money Market Fund	Mutual fund which invests in the money market which strives for a net asset value of $1 a share.
Morningstar NAV	Leading provider of information on the mutual fund industry; the dollar value of all the marketable securities (stocks, for example) owned by a mutual fund, less expenses and divided by the number of the fund's shares outstanding.
No-load Fund	A mutual fund that does not carry any commissions or sales charges (there may be administration fees).
Open-end Fund	Mutual funds that create new shares all the time as more money is invested in them.
Precious Metals Fund	Mutual funds that place a large percentage of its portfolio in gold, silver, platinum, and strategic metals by stocks, by futures, or by the valuable metals themselves.
Prospectus	A legally required document prepared by a mutual fund and sent out to potential investors that describes the fund and its operations.
Sector Fund	Mutual fund which focuses on securities of a particular industry or segment of the economy
Tax-free Fund	Mutual fund that invests the majority of its portfolio in tax-free municipal bonds and other tax exempted securities.

Retirement Plans

401(k)	Self-directed retirement plan offered to eligible employees which can choose how much and where their dollars can be invested. Employers usually match employee's contributions.
Education IRA	An IRA to which you can make tax-deferred contributions of up to $500 per year, per beneficiary, until children are 18. Withdrawals for qualified educational purposes are tax-free.
IRA	Tax-deferred retirement account which an individual can deposit up to $2,000 a year.
Keogh Plan	Tax-deferred retirement plan for self-employed people or employees of unincorporated companies that do not have their own pension plans.
Lump Sum	The entire value of an investment taken in cash at once.
Roll Over	Moving money from one retirement account into another without incurring a tax penalty; reinvestment.
Roth IRA	An IRA to which an individual can deposit up to $2,000 after-tax dollars with interest on all investments being tax-free. After 5 years, a portion of the account can be used toward buying a first-time home.
SEP	Simplified Employee Pension plan; a good retirement plan for a sole proprietor who does not have employees.
Tax-Deferred	Setting money aside that will be at a later date usually at retirement when the tax rate is lower.
Vested	Eligible to receive a pension, usually after 5 – 7 years of employment with a company.

Risk vs. Reward (1-4)

1.	Low Risk	Bank CDs, treasury bonds, treasury bills, money market funds.
2.	Limited Risk	Eligible to receive a pension, usually after 5 – 7 years of employment with a company.
3.	Moderate Risk	International investments, low-rated corporate bonds, growth stocks.
4.	High Risk	Futures, speculative stocks, high-yield bonds.

REFERENCES

Chen, James. "Bullish Engulfing Pattern." *Investopedia*, Investopedia, 19 May 2021, https://www.investopedia.com/terms/b/bullishengulfingpattern.asp.

Chen, James. "Bearish Harami Definition." *Investopedia*, Investopedia, 13 Sept. 2021, https://www.investopedia.com/terms/b/bearishharami.asp.

Mitchell, Cory. "Bearish Engulfing Pattern Definition and Tactics." *Investopedia*, Investopedia, 8 Sept. 2021, https://www.investopedia.com/terms/b/bearishengulfingp.asp.

Mitchell, Cory. "Dark Cloud Cover Definition and Example." *Investopedia*, Investopedia, 30 Dec. 2021, https://www.investopedia.com/terms/d/darkcloud.asp.

ABOUT THE AUTHOR

Ramon Singleton is a successful trader and investor in the financial markets with over 10 years' experience. His passion has led him to become an author, teacher, and mentor to many. His goal is to consistently continue to outperform the stock market year in and year out, as well as continue to outperform 401k's/ IRA's and other traditional retirement plans. He has a vision of helping individuals who are struggling financially and becoming one of the greatest traders of all time.

LET'S CONNECT

Join the Momentum Monster and learn more about stocks, trading, and investing. Scan my QR code to find various ways to connect with me!

@MomentumMonster

@momentummonster

MomentumMonster.com

For booking speaking engagements, interviews, and events, contact us at momentummonster@icloud.com.

Made in the USA
Middletown, DE
12 August 2026

30829309R00024